A ring of silver foxes,
A mist of silver foxes,
Come and sit around the hunting moon.

This edition published in 2001.

Published by Troll Communications L.L.C.

COPYRIGHT © 1990 The Rourke Corporation, Inc.
Vero Beach, Florida 32964

Text © 1990 Terri Cowman

Illustration © 1990 Charles Reasoner

LIBRARY OF CONGRESS CATALOGING-IN-PUBLICATION DATA

Cohlene, Terri, 1950-
    Little Firefly / by Terri Cohlene; illustrated by Charles Reasoner.
        p. cm. — (Native American legends)
    Summary: A retelling of the Algonquian Indian legend of how a young girl, badly mistreated by her sisters, becomes the bride of the great hunter known as the Invisible One. Includes information on the history and customs of the Algonquian Indians.
    ISBN 0-86593-005-8
        I. Algonquian Indians—Legends. 2. Algonquian Indians—Social life and customs—Juvenile literature. [1. Algonquian Indians—Legends. 2. Indians of North America — Legends. 3. Algonquian Indians—Social life and customs. 4. Indians of North America—Social life and customs.] I. Title. II. Series.
    E99.A35C68 1990
    398.22'089973—dc20   AC   CIP   89-38979

Printed in the USA

10 9 8

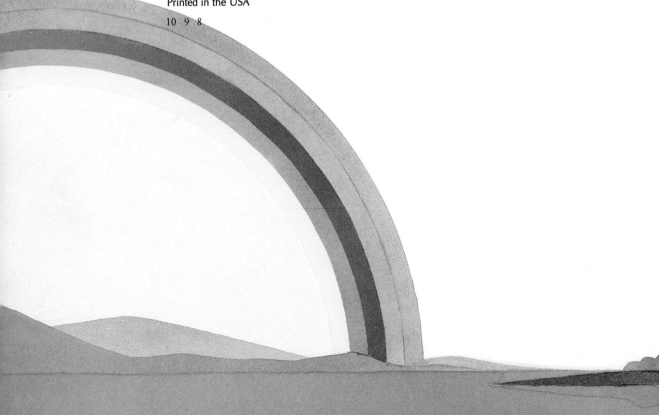

Little Firefly

AN ALGONQUIAN LEGEND

WRITTEN AND ADAPTED BY TERRI COHLENE
ILLUSTRATED BY CHARLES REASONER
DESIGNED BY VIC WARREN

Troll

Among the birches surrounding a great woodland lake, there once lived an Algonquian girl named Little Firefly. She lived in a bark wigwam with her father and two older sisters.

For days at a time, their father would hunt. "You must teach Little Firefly the skills of a woman," he would say to the older girls each time he left them.

But her sisters hated looking after Little Firefly and made her do most of the work. They often pushed her into the fire, leaving her skin puckered with scars, her hair singed and broken, her eyes red from smoke. Instead of using her name, everyone called her "Little Burnt One."

ne day, Little Firefly was mashing berries when the two older girls came up to the wigwam, arguing. "You did not see him," said the eldest. "You saw only his paddle and canoe, as I did. I guessed his bowstring was deer sinew and his hunting strap was beaver tail."

"Indeed I *did* see him," claimed the second sister. "His bowstring was twisted nettle, and his hunting strap was the neckskin of a snapping turtle! That old woman thought I was too beautiful and might make her find a wigwam of her own. That is why she sent me away."

"Who sent you away?" asked Little Firefly.

The two older sisters glanced at her. "The Invisible One and his sister, who live across the lake, if it is any business of yours."

Little Firefly knew The Invisible One was a great hunter whose guardian spirit had given him the gift of becoming invisible. He could only be seen by his sister and, one day, his bride. "Did you truly see him?" asked Little Firefly. "Are you to become his wife?"

Her sister scowled. "Why is our meal not ready, Little Burnt One?" she demanded, and pushed Little Firefly into the hot coals. Laughing, the two older girls left to gossip with the other young women in the village.

As usual, Little Firefly said nothing, but bathed her blistered feet and prepared a stew of moosemeat and corn. Then she went to sit in a grove of silver birch. The sunlight warmed her face as she softly sang to the tree spirits, asking for strength and wisdom.

Her clothing was worn and her feet were bare. If only my mother were alive, she thought. I would bathe in scented water. My dress would be of white rabbit skin, and I would wear soft moccasins decorated with quills and beads. I would braid wampum and flowers into my hair, and I could become the wife of a great hunter, perhaps even The Invisible One himself! Suddenly, she realized how long she had been daydreaming and hurried back to the wigwam.

The sisters had just finished eating the last of the stew. "Where have you been?" they asked.

"In the birch grove, talking to the tree spirits," answered Little Firefly, looking into the empty pot. "Did you not leave any for me?"

Her elder sister snorted. "And why should we, Little Burnt One? If it were not for you, we would already have husbands and wigwams. But Father will not talk of our marrying until you are old enough to be on your own!"

"I am old enough to take care of myself! I will find a husband, you will see. Then you will have to do some work yourselves!"

The sisters laughed. "Who would want an ugly Little Burnt One like you?" As they left, they called back, "We will return after the dancing tonight. Try to stay out of the fire just this once."

That night, as Little Firefly lay in her bed, she still felt the sting of her sisters' laughter. When she slept, she dreamt of silver birches swaying in the wind, and of her mother's musical voice. "Go," she whispered. "Go to the wigwam of The Invisible One. You will find much happiness."

In the morning, Little Firefly remembered her mother's words. How would I find happiness there? she wondered. I am far too ugly to be the bride of The Invisible One. Besides, none of the maidens from the village has been able to see him. How could I? Perhaps they need a servant. Surely that would be no worse than my life here.

As she picked cranberries, Little Firefly thought of the tall, handsome hunter. As she wove fishnets, she thought of his wigwam across the lake. As she gathered fresh pine boughs for the floor, she thought of a life away from her sisters. I will visit The Invisible One, she decided. But first, I must have a better dress.

15

Little Firefly once again visited the birch grove and asked the tree spirits for bark. She stripped a large piece and cut it to size, then sewed a flower design with small bits of moose hair she had saved.

She made moccasins from corn husks, and decorated her short hair with silver birch leaves. Around her neck, she wore a necklace of shells and feathers. To her waist, she tied a pouch filled with maple candy, a gift for The Invisible One. At last, she was ready.

She stepped into her own small canoe and pushed it onto the lake. As she looked over her shoulder, she saw her sisters on the shore, pointing and laughing at her. "Look," called the older girl. "Our foolish sister seeks The Invisible One!"

Little Firefly turned around and silently dipped her paddle into the water. Ahead, she saw only the lake and the forest edge. How will I know where to find him? she wondered.

The sun was settling lower and lower, painting the sky the color of chokecherries. Suddenly, she saw a curl of smoke and pointed her canoe toward it.

Soon, arriving on the beach, she was greeted by a smiling young maiden.

"Welcome. Have you come to visit my brother?" she asked.

Surely this cannot be the old woman my sisters spoke of, thought Little Firefly. "I have come," she answered, "because my mother spoke to me in a dream. She said I would find much happiness here."

The maiden held out her hand. "Follow me. My brother returns from his hunt soon. I hear his paddle in the lake. Let us find out if you can truly see him."

Little Firefly's heart fluttered. "Oh, but I did not come to seek a husband," she said. "I thought you might need help. Someone to cook for you, perhaps, or tan your animal skins."

The maiden smiled. "All the same, you must meet my brother."

They took the path through the woods until they came to a place overlooking the lake shore. Little Firefly heard water splashing against the side of a canoe. As the boat rounded into view, she gasped.

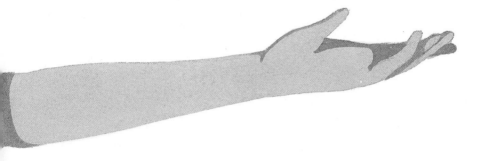

"Well, do you see him?" asked the maiden.

"I do," breathed Little Firefly. "He is indeed handsome!"

The maiden nodded. "Others before you have said so, but they did not truly see him. What is his bowstring made of?"

"Ohhhhhh! It is the rainbow!"

The maiden raised her eyebrows. "And his hunting strap?"

Little Firefly caught her breath. "It is The Star Bridge of Souls!"

The maiden smiled and took Little Firefly's hands. "You have truly seen my brother," she said. "Come. We must prepare for your meeting while he tends to his catch."

ittle Firefly covered her face with her hands. How could I have been chosen? What will he think of my scars?

When they reached the wigwam, the maiden prepared a pine-scented bath for Little Firefly. As the soothing water trickled over her, her scars disappeared.

The maiden combed sacred bear grease into Little Firefly's hair, and with each stroke, it grew longer and black as the raven's wing. The maiden braided wampum and flowers and birch leaves into Little Firefly's hair. Then she gave her a beautiful dress of white rabbit skin, and moccasins decorated with quills, shells and beads.

Little Firefly was marveling at all that had happened when she heard a lilting melody coming closer and closer to the lodge. Suddenly, the door flap was pushed aside. She gasped.

There stood The Invisible One, tall and handsome.
He lowered the love flute from his lips and smiled,
holding out his hand. "So you have come at last," he
said. "What do they call you?"

Knowing she would never again be called Little
Burnt One, she shyly placed her hand in his. "I am
named for one who carries sparks from the sun," she
replied proudly. "I am Little Firefly."

THE ALGONQUIAN

NASKAPI

CREE

MONTAGNAIS

MALISEET

QUEBEC

NEW BRUNSWICK

MICM

ONTARIO

WABANAKI

MAINE

NOVA SCOTIA

ALGONQUIN

PASSAMAQUODDY
PENOBSCOT

OJIBWAY

OTTAWA

VT.

PENNACOOK

N.Y.

N.H.

MASSACHUSET

MENOMINI

MOHAWK

WAMPANOAG

ONONDAGA

MASS.

PEQUOT

HURON

ONEIDA

CAYUGA

TUSCARORA

CT. *R.I.*

NARRAGANSET

WIS.

SENECA

MAHICAN

MICH.

POTAWATOMI

ERIE

PENN.

MONTAUK

DELAWARE

SUSQUEHANNA

N.J.

ILL.

IND.

OHIO

MD.

MIAMI

DEL.

W. VA.

VA.

POWHATAN

ALGONQUIAN INDIAN TRIBES

IROQUOIAN INDIAN TRIBES

ALGONQUIAN HOMELAND

The Algonquian homeland extends from the shores of the Great Lakes, both in what is now Canada and the United States, to the Atlantic Ocean.

Their woodland surroundings provided everything they needed: trees and shrubs for houses, clothing, cooking utensils, weapons, medicine and food. They made canoes of cedar frames, sewn together with spruce roots, covered with birchbark strips, and sealed with spruce or pine gum. The soil was fertile for farming, and the woods, lakes and streams were abundant with wildlife for food and clothing.

Villages consisted of domed or cone-shaped houses called wigwams. Single families lived in them during the winter, and often four to five families lived together during the summer months. Wigwams were constructed of bent ironwood tree frames, covered with skins, woven mats, evergreen boughs or birchbark. The bark could be rolled up and saved to use again and again when the village moved.

The interior of this Micmac wigwam was drawn in 1830. The women's caps were adapted from European styles.

ALGONQUIAN PEOPLE

"Algonquian" is from a Huron Indian word meaning "The place of spearing fish and eels from the bow of a canoe." They are a large group of people divided into smaller bands, including the Micmac, Passamaquoddy, Ojibway, Cree, Penobscot and Maliseet. They were the first Native Americans to meet the Europeans.

Men, women and children each had special duties. The men made canoes, traps, utensils and weapons. They were responsible for hunting, but it was the women who brought the game back to camp.

The women also made the clothing and wove fishnets, mats and bark containers. They gathered wild roots, nuts and berries to be made into cakes, and they collected and boiled the maple sap.

The Algonquian tribes of Maine and Nova Scotia were famous for birchbark boxes decorated with porcupine quills.

Colorful beading using floral designs became popular during the 1800s. This collar is a very fine example.

Children's main duties were to help with chores and to learn the skills they would need as adults. They often were given miniatures of adult tools, such as canoes or bows and arrows.

Like other Native Americans, the Algonquian people believed all things had a living spirit within. Everyone had a guardian spirit of their own, and it was important to pay attention to its advice.

Penobscot women's cap from the 19th century.

Ceremony was an important part of life and accompanied every important occasion. There were special songs, dances and prayers for births, deaths, the hunt, harvesting and healing. Shell belts of wampompeag, or wampum, were often exchanged as signs of good faith, and pipe-smoking carried prayers to the Great Spirit.

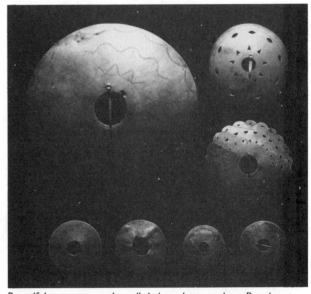

Beautiful sea curves and scroll designs decorate these Penobscot silver brooches.

Men and women shared the job of providing food for The People. Men hunted and trapped muskrat, fox, rabbit, beaver, deer and moose. Both men and women fished with spears, nets or traps. Groups living near the coast gathered shellfish.

Some tribes, like the Ojibway, raised corn, beans, tobacco and squash. Wild cranberries, blueberries and chokecherries grew nearby. With their canoes, men and women gathered wild rice. They paddled through rice patches and knocked the ripe kernels into the boats with long poles. The rice was then roasted over the fire and stored for winter in birchbark containers called mococks.

Late March was sugar season. The People collected maple sap in birchbark buckets. This was strained and cooked into sugar or syrup. They used it to season their food and make candy and beverages. Harvest and sugar times were festival times, also. A time for dancing, music and games.

Algonquian children wore nothing but moccasins in warm weather, donning fur robes during the cold. Women wore belted dresses or skirts of animal skin left open on the left side, for ease in rolling fibers against the leg to make rope or twine. They often wore nothing on top, except for a poncho or robe during cold weather.

Algonquian men wore less than the women. They were usually naked except for moccasins and a breechclout around the waist. For protection against prickly bushes in the forest, they wore leggings made by tying a piece of animal skin around the legs. In the winter, they wore robes and animal skins of moosehide.

Algonquian Indians traded with early European settlers for guns, used for hunting as well as war. This powder horn was collected in 1725.

This 19th century painting shows the "humped" canoe built by the Micmacs. The hump was for extra strength in the middle of the canoe.

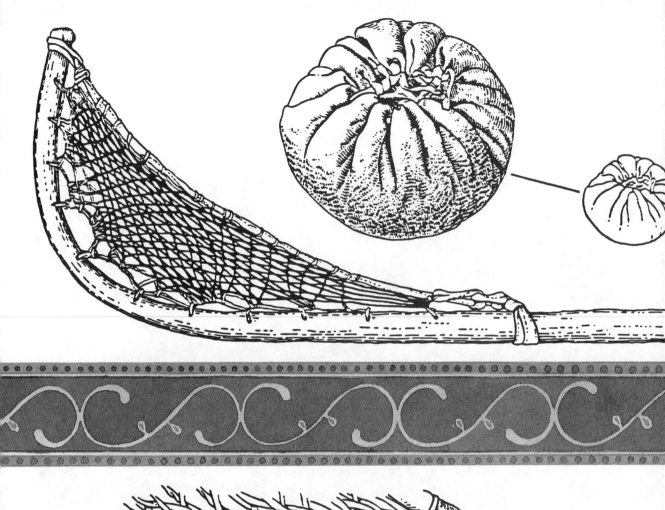

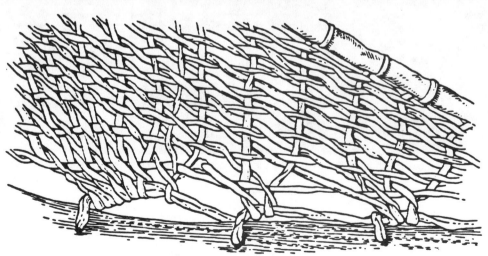

Many Algonquian tribes played lacrosse. This Passamaquoddy racket had a wooden frame and woven thong netting. The ball was of deer or moosehide.

A modern Micmac wearing traditional clothing
shows off a fine catch
during the Festival of the Forts in Nova Scotia.

ALGONQUIANS TODAY

Like most Native Americans, reservation lands were set aside for the Algonquians. Today, many still live on these lands, though few keep to all the traditional ways.

Farming, cattle ranching and tourism are examples of the professions held by present-day Algonquians. Steel-workers, teachers, lawyers and doctors are also among The People. Some live on the reservations, while others have joined the non-native population in cities and towns.

GLOSSARY

Algonquian: Huron name for native people of the Great Lakes Woodlands

Breechclout: Worn by men and boys, this soft square of leather hangs from the waist by a belt.

Leggings: A garment similar to pantlegs, tied to the belt

Mocock: Birchbark container

Sinew: Tendon found along the backbone of moose and deer, used for sewing thread

Star Bridge of Souls: The Milky Way

Wampum: Shells used for decoration, money and communication

Wigwam: Woodland people's cone- or dome-shaped house

Northern Algonquian tribes lived in cone-shaped wigwams like these. This village on Lake Huron was painted in 1845 by the famous Canadian artist, Paul Kane.

Birchbark baskets, or mococks, were decorated by cutting into the bark and peeling the top layer away.

1861-65	U.S. Civil War	**1924**	All Native Americans born in U.S. declared citizens
1890	Native Americans lose Battle of Wounded Knee, ending major Indian Wars	**1968**	Indian Civil Rights Act gives Native Americans the right to govern themselves on their reservations

One of the most useful tools of the Algonquian was the crooked knife. It was excellent for shaping and whittling, and was pulled toward the user. The man second from right in the canoe-building photo is using a crooked knife.

Even in more modern times birchbark canoes were still used for hunting and fishing. This group of Maliseets building a canoe was photographed about 1900.